Captured Ta
in German Service
Small Tanks and Armored Tractors

This French UE tractor is used by the Luftwaffe for towing aircraft bombs. Large bombs were simply attached to chains and dragged over the ground. Sometimes transport sleds made of wood were also used to move the bombs. (BA)

Werner Regenberg

Schiffer Military/Aviation History
Atglen, PA

Foreword

Some of the photos published in this book are unclear because of their original photographing technique or photo source. Because of the rarity of the photographed vehicles, these pictures have been used all the same.

The author thanks all those who have made this book possible by the free contribution of their photos. My special thanks go to my wife Astrid for her constant assistance. Any correcting and completing information in word or picture is welcome.

Dr. Werner Regenberg

Left: An armored supply carrier of Artillery Unit 227 on the chassis of an British Carrier. Since the rear bodywork was made completely new, one cannot tell whether a Bren Gun Carrier or a Scout Carrier was rebuilt. The vehicle is very neatly painted with German crosses and tactical symbols. (WS)

COVER PICTURE:
Armored Artillery Tractor per 630 (r) Komsomolyets (see page 43); drawing by Heinz Rode

Bibliography

Federal Archives, Koblenz (BA)
Military Historical Museum, Rastatt (MM)
National Archives, Washington (NA)
Tank Museum, Bovington, GB (TM)

Siegfried Borzutzki (SB)
Rudi Bahlinger (RB)
W. Bockelmann (WB)
Richard Eiermann (RE)
Wolfgang Fleischer (WF)
Gustav Haase (GH)
Randolf Kugler (RK)
Karlheinz Milch (KM)
Horst Riebenstahl (HR)
Walter Spielberger (WS)

Translated from the German by Ed Force

Copyright © 1998 by Schiffer Publishing, Ltd.

Printed in China.
ISBN: 0-7643-0573-5

This book was originally published under the title, *Waffen Arsenal-Beutepanzer Unterm Balkenkreuz* by Podzun-Pallas Verlag.

We are interested in hearing from authors with book ideas on related topics.

Published by Schiffer Publishing Ltd.
4880 Lower Valley Road
Atglen, PA 19310
Phone: (610) 593-1777
FAX: (610) 593-2002
E-mail: Schifferbk@aol.com
Please write for a free catalog.
This book may be purchased from the publisher.
Please include $3.95 postage.
Try your bookstore first.

Introduction

Service Manual D 612/1, "Heigl's Taschenbuch der Tanks", of 1935 defined the small combat vehicle as follows:

"Small combat vehicles are lightly armored, armed only with machine guns, and have modest driving capabilities. With a usually meager range, they should make possible the carrying out of their tactical reconnaissance, security and communication in armored units through their high speed and maneuverability. In other units they should serve as weapons carriers, for example, for heavy infantry weapons in the motorized infantry, or as smallest assault vehicles ("assautine") of the infantry in large-scale attacks."

The development of the small combat vehicle began in Britain, where, in the twenties, Major of the Engineers Martel and Messrs. Carden and Loyd developed armored vehicles with one- or two-man crews for the heavy infantry. The Carden-Loyd types with two-man crews were accepted, as the division of tasks between two men offered certain advantages. The Carden-Loyd Mark VI, of which 270 units were delivered between 1927 and 1930, became the "grandfather" of the small combat vehicles of many nations. The Carden-Loyd Mark VI was an armored weapons carrier for the mechanized infantry and served as an armed and partly armored towing tractor for antitank guns. The vehicle, weighing about 1.5 tons, had a two-man crew and was armed with a 7.7 mm Lewis machine gun. Its top speed was 40 kph.

As can be seen by the example of the Carden-Loyd Mark VI, the chassis of small combat vehicles, or these vehicles themselves, were also used as towing tractors or weapons carriers. On the other hand, armored, armed towing tractors often saw service in types of tasks that really called for a small combat vehicle. Small combat vehicles and lightly armored full-track tractors are therefore treated together in this book.

The Wehrmacht had no classic small combat vehicle, but began its tank development with the light Panzerkampfwagen I. In spite of this, the constant establishment of new motorized units in the Wehrmacht caused a great need for full-track towing tractors which could not be met by its own production. First experiences with small combat vehicles could be gained after the union with Austria or the occupation of Czechoslovakia, when several small combat vehicles of the Fiat-Ansaldo CV 3/33 of the Austrian Army and Czech P-I (Vz33) came into the possession of the Wehrmacht.

An abandoned UE tractor is examined by German soldiers. The transport containers of the tractor and the trailer are loaded with ammunition cases. Ahead of the transport container of the tractor, the small jack of the vehicle can be seen. (MM)

Kleinpanzer P-1 (Tancik Vz 33)

Czechoslovakia bought several Carden-Loyd Mark VI chassis from Britain in 1930, and the Ceskomoravska Kolben Danek in Prague developed them into the P-I Small Tank. The vehicle was in no way ready for the troops, and was also refused by the Army. All the same, seventy vehicles were produced in an industry-supporting move and introduced into the Army as the TANCIK Vz 33.

The vehicle had a two-man crew and was armed with two 7.92 mm ZB Vz 26 machine guns. With a maximum armor thickness of 12 mm and an overall weight of 2.5 tons, the small tank reached a speed of 35 kph.

When Czechoslovakia was occupied, several of these vehicles fell into the hands of the Wehrmacht.

Left: Members of the Panzer troops try to move a P-I Small Tank by muscle power. The vehicle was actually powered by a four-cylinder gasoline engine built by Praga, but it often broke down. The small tank still bears the typical camouflage paint pattern used on armored vehicles in the Czechoslovakian Army. (RE)

Below: Here too, its own motor is not moving it; rather it is being towed at the end of a cable. In 1933 the Czechoslovakian Army had already refused to accept further deliveries of the Vz 33 because of their bad experiences with it. The machine guns have been removed. (KM)

TK-3 and TKS (p) Small Tanks

The Polish Army bought sixteen Carden-Loyd Mark VI small tanks from Britain in 1929, as well as the rights to produce them under license, and developed the Mark VI into their own small combat vehicle, designated TK-1. The TK-1 was further developed into the TK-2 and TK-3, the latter going into series production. By 1933, some 300 TK-3 vehicles had been built and delivered to the Polish Army.

The vehicles, only 1.32 meters high, were armored with a maximum thickness of 8 mm and armed with a 7.92 mm Hotchkiss machine gun at the right front. The TK-3 small combat vehicle had a crew of two men (driver and machine gunner) and, with a weight of 2.5 tons, reached a top speed of 48 kph. The TKS successor model, introduced in 1934, had front armor increased to 10 mm, an improved machine-gun mount, and improved optical devices. The shape of the small tank's bow had also been changed. Where the TK-3 had its machine gun built into straight bow armor, the change in the TKS resulted in a balcony-like projection in which the Hotchkiss machine gun rested on a ball mount. The 40 HP Ford motor of the TK-3 was replaced by a 42 HP Polski-Fiat engine, which gave the vehicle a top speed of 40 kph. 390 of the Type TKS were built.

Toward the end of the thirties, attempts were made to improve the firepower of the TK-3 and TKS by replacing the machine gun with a 20 mm FK tank gun. This weapon had been developed for the successor model to the TKS, the 4TP Reconnaissance Tank, which could not be produced. For 1940 the rearming of 150 vehicles with the 20 mm gun was planned, and 44 of them were to be completed as soon as possible. This rearming had just been started when World War II broke out, so that only about twenty rearmed TK's were available.

A rearmored version on the chassis of the TKS was the Type C2P full-track tractor, which was used, for example, to tow the 4 cm Bofors Flak gun. In 1937, 196 of these full-track tractors were built, with another 117 ordered in 1939.

When the war broke out in September 1939, Poland had 693 vehicles of the TK-3/TKS types, of which only about 440 were ready for service. This was because a great number of the older TK type were being repaired or could no longer be repaired.

Vehicles captured by the Wehrmacht were repaired in the armored vehicle workshop in Warsaw, and some were rebuilt into towing tractors. The armored vehicle workshop in Warsaw reported in March 1941 that 55 TKS tanks were ready for service.

Two platoons of the Warsaw Light Panzer Company were equipped with TKS (p) tanks in July 1940. In September of that year, the unit was renamed Light Panzer Company East, and it saw service in Warsaw as a light armored securing unit. In 1940 the company, with its ten TKS tanks, was being used for training at the central troop training base in Warsaw; its further fate is not clear.

Other TK tanks were turned over to airfield security units of the Luftwaffe and various back-line Wehrmacht facilities, mainly in Poland.

A collecting place for Polish TK tanks. At right a TK-3 is seen from the rear, then come two TKS seen from the front, followed by a TK-3 seen from the front. The different fighting compartments and machine-gun mounts can be compared easily here. (BA)

Above: A captured TK-3 tank, here loaded onto a Polski-Fiat 621 L transport truck. For longer road trips, the TK tanks were loaded onto trucks that were especially equipped for this task. (WS)

Below: A rear view of a TK-3, now owned by the Military Museum of Belgrade. The vehicle must have made its way to Yugoslavia with the German Wehrmacht. On the right side of its body is a fork mount to which a machine gun could be attached for anti-aircraft defense. A Polish towing hook is attached to the rear of the body. (RK)

Left: TK-3 tanks in a motor pool of the 1st Panzer Division shortly after the Polish campaign. The Panzerkampfwagen IV, Type A, behind the small tank belongs to the second unit of Panzer Regiment 2. The straight front of the TK-3 with the small balcony for the machine-gun mount can be seen clearly. (GH)

Right: The 1st Panzer Division also had a TKS tank in its motor pool. Several soldiers have gathered around the weaponless tank for a souvenir photo. Panzer III tanks can be seen in the background. (HR)

Left: In Norway in the winter of 1943-44, a TKS tank serves as a towing tractor for a 37 mm Pak gun. There are no good seating possibilities for the gun crew on the towing vehicle, which was surely uncomfortable on long marches. The vehicle belonged to a securing unit of the Luftwaffe. (BA)

Above: Rear view of a TKS tank, abandoned by its crew somewhere in Poland. In comparison to the TK-3, the body is shaped somewhat differently (with more angled flat surfaces). The TKS were built with only one rack for a spare road wheel on the rear, where the TK-3 had a rack for two spare road wheels. (KM)

Below: TNK small tanks in use during the filming of a propaganda film for the Wehrmacht. The tanks have a screen camouflage pattern that varies from one vehicle to another. The 7.92 mm Hotchkiss machine guns are still installed in the ball mantlets. (BA)

Above: This TKS has been rearmed with a German 7.92 mm MG 15 with circular sight. Other than the weapon and the German crew, no German emblems or tactical symbols indicate its ownership by the Wehrmacht. (RE)

Below: A few TKS were still in use with the Wehrmacht until the war ended, as this photo shows. An American soldier is inspecting a TKS tank near Bitsch, France, on March 17, 1945. The vehicle is marked with German crosses on the rear viewing hatch and on the sides of the body. (NA)

TKS tanks of the Light Panzer Company East in a 1940 parade in Warsaw, marking the first anniversary of the capture of Warsaw. The small tanks are marked with very large German crosses on the bow, and with small three-digit tactical numbers on the sides. (BA)

Below: TKS tanks of the Light Panzer Company East on maneuvers. The crewman at the front of the vehicle wears the protective Panzer cap along with his Panzer uniform, and is using an indicator to signal for a left turn. The TKS tanks have been rearmed with German MG 34 guns. (WB)

Left: A TKS tank fitted with a 20 mm FK gun is examined by Wehrmacht men. The vehicles were very eye-catching when fitted with the long gun and the large ball mantlet. The TKS with the 20 mm gun was a serious challenger to the German Panzer I and II tanks. (KM)

Right: The long 20 mm gun has been removed from this TKS. A periscope for the aiming gunner remains, mounted on the roof of the vehicle.

Below: The unarmored version of the TKS was the C2P full-track tractor, which was used as a towing vehicle for the Polish 4 cm Bofors Flak gun. Here is such a vehicle in Luftwaffe service during or shortly after the Polish campaign, as the white German cross shows. (BA)

Vickers-Armstrong VA 601 (b) Armored Full-Track Tractor

The Belgian Army looked for a suitable towing vehicle for their 47 mm Pak, which had been introduced as their standard antitank weapon. They experimented with the Vickers-Carden-Loyd Mark VI, a half dozen of which were brought in from Britain in 1930. They decided, though, on a full-track tractor made by the Vickers firm, the Vickers Utility B Type, for which Belgian production rights were obtained in 1934.

In 1935, the first deliveries of the "Tracteur chenille Vickers-Carden-Loyd Utility", as the vehicle was called, arrived. The small tractors, 2.42 meters long, 1.63 meters high and equally wide, attained a top speed of 32 kph. With a maximum armor of 8 mm, the vehicle weighed barely two tons.

The full-track tractor was delivered in two versions, one each for the infantry and cavalry. Both versions were used as towing tractors for the 47 mm Pak guns.

The infantry model had only one driver, while the cavalry type had a three-man crew. The vehicles looked very much the same, differing in a straight upper rear angle for the infantry version, while this panel was rounded on the cavalry version to allow space for the seats of the two additional crewmen. They sat with their backs to the driver.

By March 1936, 177 infantry tractors and 85 of the cavalry version had been delivered from Vickers of Britain.

From this time on, building under license began at the Familleureux Iron Works in Belgium, but an improved version was built. The body was lengthened and the track extent enlarged, simultaneously increasing the track.

In all versions, the driver's position was protected by folding sheets of armor. A large number of the more than 300 utility tractors well into the hands of the Wehrmacht

and were usually used as towing tractors for medium and heavy antitank guns. Several vehicles of the Familleureux type were converted for use as explosives carriers and used by Panzer Unit 300 (Fl.) (see also Weapon Arsenal Special Volume 10). Photos show that they were also used by the Luftwaffe, for example, as aircraft towing tractors.

In October 1939, fifty Vickers-Carden-Loyd Utility vehicles were ordered from the Familleureux works in Belgium by The Netherlands for the Royal Netherlands Indian Army (KNIL). Twenty vehicles were to be delivered by mid-April and the remaining thirty by mid-May 1940. In December 1939, there came an order for thirty more vehicles, which were to be delivered in June 1940. The first twenty vehicles presumably all reached the Royal Netherlands Indian Army, but the other sixty fell into German hands or were finished in the time of German occupation.

The vehicles built for the KNIL, unlike the Belgian types, had folding sidewalls, through the use of which seating for a six-man gun crew could be created. The folding armor plates that protected the driver had been eliminated. These full-track tractors were also used to tow antitank guns, as well as infantry guns.

The Fast Unit 198 of the 98th Infantry Division stated in an experience report of September 1942:

"Vickers-Armstrong with an engine output of 54 HP developed a top soeed of 40 kph. The condition of the motors is bad, thus high oil consumption. In some cases connecting rods and crankshafts or their bearings had to be replaced. Because of the heavy gun (75 mm Pak, author's note), off-road steering is very hard. Driving in hilly terrain can be done only with the greatest care, since the tractor tips very easily. Fuel consumption: 100 liters per 100 kilometers (gasoline). Oil: 4-5 liters per 100 km."

Members of the 1st Panzer Division, seen during the western campaign with a Utility Tractor produced at the Familleureux works in Belgium. The track is widened, as the tracks have been moved all the way out, and the track length has been increased, meaning that the distance between the leading wheel and the last road wheel has been extended. All in all, the vehicles appear somewhat weightier than those made by Vickers. (HR)

Driving tests with a captured Utility Tractor on October 31, 1940, at the Army Motor Pool in Gient, Belgium. This was the infantry version of the vehicle produced in Britain. The vehicle is marked WH, thus chearly belonging to the Army branch of the Wehrmacht. (BA)

The same vehicle with its armor plates folded up to protect the driver, pulling a full-track trailer such as was developed for the French UE tractor. There are no seats for anyone other than the driver. Loads could be stowed on the tractor to the right and left of the engine. (BA)

Here is the cavalry version, made in Britain, of the Utility Tractor pulling a 75 mm Pak 40. The handholds and footrests on the rounded rear for the two crewmen sitting backward can be seen clearly. But these two seats were not enough for the five-man crew of the antitank gun, so that a somewhat different seating order had to be used. (BA)

This Utility Tractor, produced at the Familleureux works, saw service with the 3./Panzerjäger Unit 131 in Russia. The tractor is towing a 75 mm Pak 41 and clearly shows the disadvantage of not having enough seats for the gun crew. It was surely not easy for the crew to keep a firm hold of the vehicle in rough country. (BA)

A Vickers-Armstrong Tractorm built for the KNIL at Familleureux, in action on Crete as a tractor for a 5 cm Pak 38. The gun crew had plenty of seating space to the right and left of the motor on this model. The one remaining disadvantage of the small tractor was the lack of space for ready ammunition.

Below: This Vickers-Armstrong tractor of the "KNIL" type is being used to transport sacks of field mail. The sidewalls, now folded up, could fold down to provide seats for the passengers. The vehicle is equipped with German Notek camouflage headlights.

Armored Ammunition Tractor UE 630 (f)

As did other nations, France also bought the Carden-Loyd Mark VI, and the Latil firm obtained the production license. The Renault firm also took part in a competition for an armored supply vehicle, and received a contract to build these vehicles, based on the Latil Tracteur N. The vehicle, officially known as the Renault Chenillette d'Infanterie Type UE, was put into service by the French Army in 1931.

The vehicles, only 1.25 meters high, 1.74 m wide and 2.80 m long, had armor up to 9 mm thick and no weapons. They had two-man crews and, with a weight of 2.64 tons, attained a top speed of 30 kph.

The little vehicles could move a payload of 400 kg in a container located at the rear of the body. The container could be removed from the vehicle automatically and emptied. Another load og 500 kg could be carried in a full-track trailer developed for the tractor.

In 1937 the improved UE 2 Version (or Model 1937) appeared, equipped with a gearbox that had four instead of the previous three forward speeds. From the outside, the two versions can scarcely be told from each other. By the beginning of the war or the French surrender, some 5000 vehicles of the Renault UE (Model 1931) and UE 2 (Model 1937) had been built.

The UE tractors were used in the French Army not only as ammunition carriers, but also as towing tractors for 25 mm antitank guns.

The Wehrmacht captured some 3000 UE tractors and had them overhauled in an assembly plant at Paris-Issy les Moulineaux under the direction of the M.A.N. firm. These vehicles were given their own service designations, which were translations of their original French names. Their designations were:

D 628/25   Armored ammunition tractor UE (f) and trailer UE (f). Equipment description and service manual of 11/18/41.

D 628/29   Armored ammunition tractor UE (f) and trailer UE (f). Chassis lubrication and servicing manual of 10/15/41.

Since the development of a German ammunition carrier (Borgward) made only slow progress, the Wehrmacht considered the possibility of resuming production of the Renault UE. But since the machines had been rebuilt for other production and the expenditure of raw materials could not be compared with the value of the vehicles, the plans were dropped.

The evaluation of the Renault UE and its use in the German Army can be seen best in the following excerpt from a report of the General of the Infantry to the Army High Command in December 1942:

1. TECHNICAL DETAILS:

Product: Renault "Chenillette"
Type: Armored ammunition carrier full-track vehicle (rebuilt tank)
Engine: Gasoline, 38 HP, 2120 cc displacement
Speed: On-road: to 25 kph; off-road: to 15 kph
Fuel consumption: On-road 45-60 liters, off-road 70-100 ltr.
Tank capacity: 56 liters
Inherent weight: 2600 kg
Load limit: 300-1500 kg, depending on terrain
Pulling power: 500-1500 kg, depending on terrain
Armor plate: withstands rifle shots & light splinters

2. USES:

a. Towing light infantry gun, 37 mm Pak & Spl. Trl. 32
b. Towing 50 mm Pak, 75 mm, 76.2 mm & heavy infantry guns
c. Transporting position material and seated wounded
d. Towing service
e. Self-propelled mount for installed 37 mm Pak
f. Scout car with installed machine gun
g. Ammunition carrier +/- trailer to arm gun positions

3. ADVANTAGES:

The "Chenillette" is very handy, has sufficient ground clearance, offers a small target and handles roughest terrain. For short scouting missions it is useful and can be used to transport ammunition etc. and move light guns into even the most advanced positions. Its armor secures it against rifle fire and light splinters. Because of its low height, it offers armor-piercing weapons only a very small target.

By attaching an appropriate TRACKED TRAILER to the Chenillette, its transport capacity is increased significantly.

4. DISADVANTAGES:

a. Mechanically, the "Chenillette" is very sensitive, has a weak engine that becomes hot easily, consumes too much fuel, and produces loud noises. The cooling is not sufficient.
b. Driver's and passenger's seats are too narrow.
c. Because of too low speed and high fuel consumption, it can only be used for short distances and cannot stand long marches.

d. Because of too stiffly sprung road wheels, the vehicle shakes badly. Many breakdowns result from spring breakage and track damage.

e. The badly chosen gear ratios in the gearbox result in overrevving and thus overheating of the engine.

f. Because of its short body and resulting tipping movements, it is not suited for carrying lying wounded.

The uses of the UE tractor listed in the report above, though, do not give a complete overview. Further possible uses of the vehicle included carrying explosives (see Weapon Arsenal Special Volume 10), serving as a self-propelled mount for 28/32 cm launchers, chassis for dummy tanks, and several other uses.

A significant rebuilding was the Renault UE reconnaissance tank. By the Becker building staff, 24 tractors were equipped with an armored rear body in which radio equipment and observation personnel were housed. Several of these vehicles were used by the 21st Panzer Division.

The Luftwaffe used the Renault UE at its airfields and field airstrips as tractors for towing aircraft, bomb sleds and other equipment.

The Luftwaffe also rebuilt UE tractors into genuine small tanks used for securing its airfields and bases. By installing machine guns behind shields and in armored balconies, small series of securing vehicles, or individual ones, were created.

Left: Not all the captured tractors were in usable condition; some were very badly damaged and not worth repairing. The usable components were removed from such vehicles as spare parts, and the rest was scrapped. (KM)

Right: Repaired UE tractors at a motor pool. In the center is a UE 2 (1937 model), flanked by two 1931 model UE machines. In comparison to the satanding soldier, the flat design of the tractors can be seen clearly. (KM)

A column of Renault Chenillettes in use as ammunition tractors. The transport containers are filled with ammunition cases. All the vehicles are marked with WH number plates (in front, WH-1223800) and German crosses. (BA)

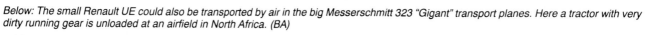

Below: The small Renault UE could also be transported by air in the big Messerschmitt 323 "Gigant" transport planes. Here a tractor with very dirty running gear is unloaded at an airfield in North Africa. (BA)

A Renault Chenillette with a captured limber trailer from a Russian 45 mm Pak gun in tow, driving through a city in Crimea (probably Sevastopol). A third soldier has found himself a seat in the container. The lack of space for more passengers along with the crew was a big problem for these small tractors. Beside the tractor is a Command Tank III of Panzer Unit 300 (Fl). (BA)

Below: The problem of space for passengers could, though, be solved sufficiently, as this photo shows. The Renault UE is towing a gun trailer and three typical farm trailers. More than twenty soldiers and their equipment were transported this way. (BA)

A Renault tractor is used to tow a 37 mm Pak gun in France. In the container, the tractor carries ammunition and equipment. The tracked trailer transports the gun crew and more equipment, and its cover offers some protection from the rainstorm. The gun brings up the rear. (BA)

Below: The cramped seats and the use of all free space on the vehicle are shown here. The UE tractors are being used to tow 5 cm Pak guns. In the container are ammunition cases, and pieces of equipment are all over the vehicle. (BA)

With larger and heavier guns, such as this 75 mm Pak 97/38, the pulling power of the tractor was not sufficient to tow a trailer for the gun crew as well. The gun crew had to move to another vehicle, such as a truck. There were often problems because of the different speeds and off-road capabilities of the vehicles. (BA)

Below: Renault tractors were also used to tow the heavy 7.62 cm Pak 36. With the road conditions shown here, the gun crew could only follow on foot or in a vehicle with off-road capability. (BA)

By installing a machine gun, the unarmed tractors were made into armed reconnaissance vehicles. The possibility of mounting an MG 34 with a central brace at the center of the tractor was already known in the French campaign. The machine-gun mount is lashed in place, and the gunner sits in the container. (MM)

Below: Side view of the same UE tractor, here providing armed transportation with a trailer. The containers could hold food canisters. (MM)

Left: Th...
being u...
curity...
drawn...
armec...
MG Z...
magazines. ...
tractor has been rebuilt clev...
erly as a mount for the machine gun.

Below: Another step in remodeling into an armed vehicle involves installing a shield, as on this vehicle. The two gunners who operate the sMG 34 are both completely protected by the big shield, which may have come from an antitank gun. (BA)

The Luftwaffe also used Renault Chenillettes for a variety of transport and towing tasks. This UE tractor is bringing the crew of a Messerschmitt 210 to their aircraft. (BA)

Below: Other than the crew's Luftwaffe uniforms, nothing marks this tractor as having been captured by the Wehrmacht. The driver has equipped his compartment with the bubble of an airplane as a windshield. No other means of transportation seems to be available for the case that is being towed on a line. (BA)

This UE-2 was rebuilt into a heavily armed vehicle. Three MG 15 have been mounted on the Renault. The machine guns in front of the passenger seat and the container have been equipped with steel shields. (WF)

Below: In this side view, the positions of the three guns can be seen clearly. In front, the MG with a ball mantlet is on a plain armor plate; the middle MG also has a ball mantlet and is on an armor plate, but here a complete fighting position has been built up with wooden blocks and sheet metal. The rear MG has been mounted for anti-aircraft use. (WF)

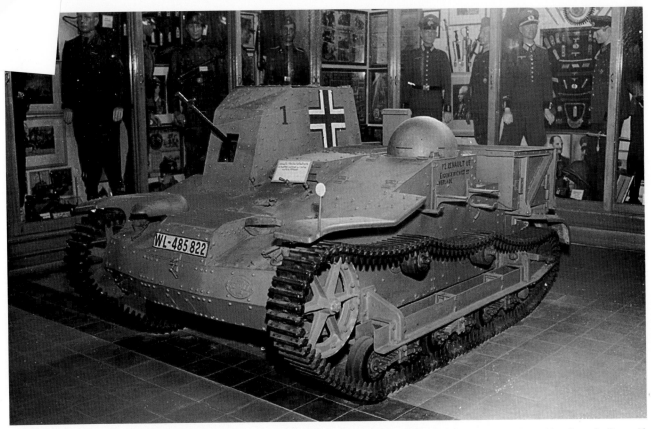

This Luftwaffe security vehicle on Renault UE chassis is in the Belgian Army Museum in Brussels. The passenger's seat has been built up with armor plate and turned into a real machine-gun position. The vehicle is armed with an MG 81.

Below: This former Luftwaffe security vehicle is in the Army Museum in Copenhagen. In addition to one type of MG mount for the passenger, there is a second mount for an MG 15 or 81 in the place of the transport container. These security vehicles were rebuilt by local troops as suggested by Army officials, and thus very varied. There were also a few small series of them. (RB)

Left: To train antitank soldiers, dummy tanks that looked like the most varied enemy tanks were built by the replacement and training units of the Wehrmacht and mounted on all sorts of chassis. This dummy represents the Russian T-34 tank and is mounted on a Renault UE chassis. (WS)

Right: During the French campaign the troops realized that a combination of the UE tractor and the 37 mm Pak made a simple, effective self-propelled gun. This Pak, wheels and all, is mounted on the track aprons and secured against slipping with ropes and branches. The markings identify the tractor and Pak as Wehrmacht vehicles. (SB)

Left: The 14th Company of the Engineer Training Regiment built wooden "shoes" to hold the wheels of a 37 mm Pak on the track aprons. The company's last UE tractor was put out of action on July 29, 1941 and was given a "vehicle burial". (RK)

27

For permanent service as a self-propelled gun, the 37 mm Pak was attached to the Renault tractor with its mount but without wheels or spars. The gun crew found more or less comfortable space to operate the gun in the transport container, plus enough storage space for ammunition. Several infantry divisions rebuilt their Renault tractors as self-propelled guns in this way. (TM)

Below: A 37 mm Pak mounted on a Renault UE armored artillery tractor in service with the 125th Infantry Division at Rostov. The seating order of the gun crew is clear. At right, Knight's Cross Bearer Oberstleutnant Reinhardt stands next to the vehicle.

To strengthen artillery firepower in fighting off an Allied invasion in France early in 1944, this UE tractor was fitted with launchers for 28/32 cm rockets. To point the vehicle at the target, a makeshift aiming device was installed in front of the driver. This photo shows Field Marshal Rommel inspecting such a vehicle. (BA)

Below: Another version of the Renault tractor with launchers for 28/32 cm rockets mounted on its sides. The rocket attachments are the same type as was used on Sd. Kfz. 251. The aiming device is folded down on the right vehicle and missing from the left one. (NA)

A Renault UE tractor of the artillery unit of the 227th Infantry Division, equipped to lay field cables. The cables could be laid from the slowly moving vehicle. Several cable drums could be carried in the transport container. (WS)

Below: This Renault trailer was rebuilt as an artillery observation tank. The armored upper body, replacing the container, provided room for the observation personnel and their equipment. 24 such observation tanks were built. (WS)

Armored MG Carrier 731 (e) (Bren Carrier)

From the Carden-Loyd series of the thirties (see the introduction), a light armored vehicle was developed in Britain to carry a machine gun and its crew safely and nimbly, even under fire. From this requirement and the Bren machine gun came the vehicle's name of "Bren Carrier" for the entire later developmental series.

Although the Bren Carrier was not actually an armored fighting vehicle, but rather an armored weapons or personnal transporter, the vehicles were listed on the Wehrmacht's Foreign Equipment List in the 700 series of "Panzerkampfwagen".

The Bren Carrier had a three-man crew; next to the driver (at right front) sat the machine gunner on the left, operating the forward-mounted MG, and behind him on the left, next to the engine, was a seat for another man, who sometimes operated a second Bren gun. Often there was a Boys antitank gun mounted in the front in place of the machine gun.

These vehicles, 1.45 meters high, 2.05 m wide and 3.66 m long, were armored with, at most, 10 mm plates. With a fighting weight of 3.75 tons, they attained a top speed of 48 kph.

Bren Carriers saw service with the British Expeditionary Corps in France and Belgium; every infantry division was supposed to have 96 of them. The total number of Bren Carriers that saw service with the Expeditionary Corps is not known, nor is the number of these vehicles captured by the Wehrmacht. In all, over 1000 Bren carriers were built in Britain between 1941 and 1943, plus another 5500 in Australia and New Zealand.

Bren Carriers were utilized by the Wehrmacht as full-tracked tractors, explosive carriers (see Weapon Arsenal Special Volume 10), and small battle tanks to secure Luftwaffe airfields.

The Schmitt firm carried out tests with plow blades built onto Bren Carriers. Bren Carriers with blades are said to have been used by the Luftwaffe to remove snow from their airstrips.

For the Artillery Regiment of the 227th Infantry Division, several Bren Carriers were rebuilt as supply and ammunition carriers. The rebuilding was done to suggestions by the battery chief of the 15./Art. Reg. 227, Hauptmann Becker.

Left: A parked Bren Carrier somewhere in the West. The white-painted square was a British recognition mark that was painted on all their armored vehicles in France. All the Bren Carrier's weapons have been removed. (KM)

Right: This vehicle was turned over to the Army Weapons Office after the French campaign. Typical of the Bren Carrier is the angled fighting compartment for the third crewman on the left side of the vehicle.

The Luftwaffe used Bren Carriers similarly to the French Renault Chenillettes for towing tasks of all kinds on their airfields. This Carrier is being used to tow heavy bombs in Sicily. (BA)

Below: The Schmidt firm carried out tests by mounting plow blades on captured Bren Carriers. The Luftwaffe is said to have used Bren Carriers with blades to remove snow from airstrips. (BA)

Armored MG Carrier 732 (e) (Scout Carrier)

A variant of the Bren Carrier was the Scout Carrier developed for the cavalry regiments of the motorized divisions. The Scout Carrier was used as a weapon carrier for the Boys antitank gun, which was mounted on the bow of the vehicle in place of a machine gun. At the right rear, beside the motor, and thus unlike the Bren Carrier, there was room for two more gunners, and there was storage space for equipment at the left rear of the vehicle.

The Scout Carrier also had mounts for a Bren machine gun in the rear fughting compartment. There were 667 of these vehicles built.

The vehicles, 1.59 meters high, 2.05 m wide and 3.66 m long, bore armor at most 10 mm thick. With a fighting weight of 3.75 tons, they reached a top speed of 48 kph, and thus scarcely differed from the Bren Carrier in technical terms.

Each of seven cavalry regiments in the British Expeditionary Corps went to France and Belgium with 44 Scout Carriers.

Scout Carriers captured by the Wehrmacht were used as were the Bren Carriers. One particular modification was the self-propelled mount designated "3.7 cm Pak on MG Carrier (Vickers Bren Carrier)", a vehicle that was used for training on self-propelled gun mounts by Panzerjäger Replacement and Training Unit 33 in Landau. Here too, confusion in the designation of a Scout Carrier as a Bren Carrier occurs, as the entire family of vehicles was known under the name of Bren Carrier.

Left: An abandoned Scout Carrier somewhere in France. Unlike the Bren Carrier, the Scout Carrier had its fighting compartment on the right side of the engine. (KM)

Right: A Bren Carrier (center) and a Scout Carrier (right) in a Wehrmacht motor pool. The differences in the bodies of the Bren and Scout Carriers can be seen clearly. In front of the Carriers are an Austro-Daimler ADMK-WARK and a Renault UE tractor.

A Scout Carrier used by a security unit of the Luftwaffe in the Scandinavian area. At least fourteen soldiers have found room on the vehicle. To the left of the Scout Carrier is a Bren Carrier. All the vehicles bear white winter camouflage. (BA)

Below: A Scout Carrier by the name of "Boy", with a crew of Luftwaffe men. On the armor plate above the machine gun, the lettering says: "Repaired, ready to go, water discharged, battery connected". (KM)

Above and below: The 3.7 cm self-propelled Pak of Panzerjäger Replacement Unit 33 in Landau/Pfalz, based on the Scout Carrier. Since not enough self-propelled guns were available for training purposes, these self-propelled guns were used to meet the need. The vehicle was designated "3.7 cm Pak on MG Carrier (Vickers Bren Carrier)". To create a fighting compartment for the gun crew, a wall of wood was mounted on the left side.

This armored ammunition carrier of Artillery Unit 227 used the Bren or Scout Carrier chassis. The rear fighting compartment was rebuilt and attachments for the cover were welded on. The ammunition trailer was made of French components. (WS)

Armored Machine Gun Carrier (e) (Universal Carrier)

Further derivatives of the Bren Carrier were a Cavalry Carrier, which could transport six soldiers in addition to the driver and machine gunner, and an armored observation vehicle (Carrier Armoured OP) for the artillery. Fifty of the Cavalry Carrier and 95 of the observation vehicle were built.

In order to simplify the variety of types, as of 1940 only the basic vehicle, the Universal Carrier, was built and modified slightly to suit all needs. The body of the Universal Carrier was a combination of the Bren and Scout Carriers, with a fighting compartment on either side of the engine, while the front part remained unchanged. The fighting compartment to the right of the engine provided space for the third member of the crew, while that at left held equipment or other personnel. The main armament in the bow was still a Bren machine gun or a Boys antitank gun. Among the troops the vehicles were still known usually as Bren Carriers, regardless of their armament.

Their technical data were the same as those of the Scout Carrier, while weapons and equipment suited their purposes.

In Great Britain alone, over 30,000 Universal Carriers were built, with a similar number produced in Canada and others built in Australia and New Zealand. As of 1940, the Universal Carrier could be found in all theaters of war. 2550 of them were also delivered to Russia, 1212 of these made in Britain and 1348 in Canada.

The Universal Carriers captured by the Wehrmacht, like the Brens and Scouts, were used as towing tractors, transport and supply vehicles.

The 3rd Panzergrenadier Division set up a tank destroyer company in 1944, using twelve Universal Carriers. Four vehicles were armed with MG 42 guns, equipped with Panzerfaust and radio, and used as command cars, while eight others carried three Panzerschreck antitank rockets and five Panzerfaust weapons each. All the Carriers were fitted with racks for twelve ammunition cases for Panzerbüchse rockets on the rear.

The 9th Infantry Division reported in an experience report of November 1942:

"In this division there are, in addition (to the Renault UE; author's note), two captured Ammunition Tractors Mark I of British origin (Bren Carriers; author's note). This tractor offers better potential for carrying gunners, attains high speeds (Ford V-8 engine), and runs almost soundlessly. The Mark I is also far superior to the Renault tractor in all technical details and in quality. Very well suited for advanced units."

A captured Universal Carrier is used for transportation by German mountain troops in Crete. The Universal Carrier was basically a combination of the Bren and Scout Carriers. (BA)

Below: Three Universal Carriers in a German Wehrmacht parade in a Greek city. The Bren Carrier could be used as an armored personnel carrier, similarly to the halftrack SPW Sd. Kfz. 250. (KM)

A captured Bren Carrier used by the Brandenburgers in the vicinity of Benghazi in 1942. Note the extended track protectors, which were used mainly in Africa to decrease dust penetration. (RK)

Below: Another Universal Carrier of the Brandenburgers, also near Benghazi in 1942. The vehicle, also with extended track protectors, has been rebuilt as a self-propelled mount for a heavy Panzerbüchse 41. (RK)

A Universal Carrier company troop vehicle in a tank destroyer company of the 3rd Panzergrenadier Division in Italy in 1944. The vehicle is armed with a bow MG 42 and carries Panzerfaust devices in its rear compartment. At the rear are racks with ammunition cases for Panzerbüchse 54 rockets. (BA)

Below: Tank destroyer vehicles of the 3rd Panzergrenadier Division in Italy. The Universal Carriers were each armed with three Panzerbüchse 54 rockets and several Panzerfaust devices. At the rear were twelve ammunition cases for Panzerbüchse rockets. (BA)

Small Tank T 32 (j) (Skoda 36)

The Czech firm of Skoda built prototypes of a small tank with the type designations S-1-d and T-2 D in 1936. The two-men crews had a 3.7 cm tank gun and a 7.92 cm ZB Vz 26 machine gun as their weapons. With a fighting weight of 3.9 tons, the vehicles reached a top speed of 40 kph. The heaviest armor plate was 20 mm thick. The vehicles were 1.63 meters high, 2 meters wide and 3.7 meters long. The T-2 D prototype was followed by a small T-3 D series, eight of which were delivered to Yugoslavia, where they bore the designation T-32.

The vehicles were captured by the Wehrmacht in Yugoslavia, and one of them was carried by Armored Train Belgrad of Pz.Kp. z.b.V. 12 as Skoda 36 in 1941.

Left: Skoda built prototypes of this small tank in 1936, with the designation S-1-d and T-2 D. Eight of this type, with a 3.7 cm tank gun and a MG, were used by the Yugoslav Army as T-32. (WS)

Below: At this collection point in Kragoyevac in June 1941 are not only a dozen Yugoslav FT 17 tanks but also one of the eight T-32s. A captured T-32 small tank was used in November 1941 by Pz.Kp. z.b.V. 12 and designated Skoda 36. (BA)

Armored Artillery Tractor 630 (r)

On the basis of a request from the Soviet Army leadership for a tractor to tow the 45 mm antitank gun, the Moskauer Traktorenwerk Zavod No. 37 developed a completely new vehicle. The Komsomolyets Artillery Tractor was the only partly armored Soviet towing tractor. The artillery tractor had an armored cab for the driver on the left and a machine gunner on the right. The 7.6 mm DT machine gun was mounted in a ball mantlet in the front plate. Behind the armored cab were three folding seats on each side for the gun crew. These seats could be protected from the weather by a canvas, but there was no armor plate. The vehicle was 1.4 meters high, 1.84 m wide and 3.4 m long, and its thickest armor was 16 mm. With a weight of four tons, the tractor attained a top speed of 40 kph.

Between 1937 and 1941, 4401 Komsomolyets tractors were built. An improved 1938 model, with a more powerful engine and modified machine-gun mount, was made in only small numbers in comparison to the 1937 standard type.

The Komsomolyets tractors captured by the Wehrmacht were used as supply carriers or as towing tractors for heavy antitank and artillery guns.

Left: An abandoned Komsomolyets tractor found by the 290th Infantry Division. The tractor is missing two road wheels, and its gun has been removed, ball mantlet and all. To make such captured vehicles ready for use again required a lot of effort by the repair services. (KM)

Below: A Komsomolyets tractor as an ammunition and supply carrier of the 2nd Company, Panzerjäger Unit 134. The tactical symbols of the Panzerjäger Company and the 134th Infantry Division can be seen clearly on the Sd. Anh. 32 being towed by the tractor. The large German cross on the hatch covers of the armored cab is also easy to see. (KM)

Two 1937 model Komsomolyets tractors are being towed here by a captured STZ-3 full-track tractor. The more of such tractors that were available, the more easily usable vehicles could be repaired by using parts from other tractors. (BA)

Below: The STZ 630 (r) armored artillery tractor of the 267th Infantry Division. This was the improved 1938 model with a modified machine-gun position, of which only a smaller number than the standard 1937 model were built. Alonig with German crosses and division markings, this vehicle bears WH (Wehrmacht Heer) lettering.

A 630 (r) armored artillery tractor, with its 7.6 mm DT MG in the bow, is fully ready for action. It looks as if the crew has gathered fir trees for Christmas. The German crosses on the bow and sides are very narrow (see cover picture). (BA)

Below: A Komsomolyets tractor in a German city, followed by a Hitler Youth band and a marching group. The vehicle has German crosses on the front plate and hatch covers. The 1937 model of the Komsomolyets tractor was made with the angular visor covers shown here and with rounded ones.

A Komsomolyets tractor with a German cross on the rear and rounded visor covers. Behind the tractor is a 4.5 cm Pak 37 (r) with a limber trailer, a gun developed out of the German 3.7 cm Pak. On the left in the photo is the rear of a vehicle of Propaganda Company 621, which presumably also took this picture. (BA)

Below: Not only the tractor seen here is captured, but so is the gun in tow. The Russian 76 mm 1936 cannon (F-22) was used in large numbers by the Wehrmacht with the designation 7.62 Field Gun 296 (r). (HS)

On a dusty airstrip, this Armored Artillery Tractor 630 (r) pulls a light 10.5 cm Field Howitzer 18. On the rear of the tractor there was room for the gun crew and pieces of equipment. (BA)

Below: With a lot of work, this Komsomolyets tractor was turned into a self-propelled mount for a 3.7 cm Pak gun. The gun has been mounted on the armored cab and has a wide shield to protect the gun crew, for whom extra seating was also provided. Since the hatches could no longer be used because of the gun on top, the left sidewall has been rebuilt as a door, which is standing open here. As the four score rings indicate, the rebuilding was worthwhile. (WS)

Panzerkampfwagen L 3/33 731 (i)

Italy also procured several Carden-Loyd Mark VI in 1929, as well as a license to produce them. The Fiat-Ansaldo CV 29 built under license was further developed into the Type CV 3/33 small tank, followed in 1935 by the Type CV 3/35. The two types doffered only in a few minor details, and had as their primary weapons two coaxial 8 mm Fiat Model 35 or Breda Model 38 machine guns. In 1938 several more vehicles were produced with modifiede running gear as the L 3.38. Likewise in 1938 the designations CV (Carro Veloce) 3/33 and 3/35 were changed to L 3/33 and 3/35.

The vehicles were 1.28 meters high, 1.4 m wide and 3.2 m long, had a two-man crew, and bore armor plate up to 13.5 mm thick. With a weight of 3.2 tons, they reached a top speed of 42 kph.

In all, about 2500 L 3 tanks were produced, including a flamethrowing version. The L 3 was also exported from Italy; for example, 74 Type 3/33 and 3/35 units went to Austria. The 74 L 3 tanks on hand in Austria were taken over by the Wehrmacht in 1938 and used by Panzer Regiment 33 as its first tanks. After Panzer Regiment 33 was rearmed with Panzer I and II tanks, the L 3 tanks were used for training purposes, some at the School for Army Motorization in Wünsdorf. Nine vehicles were used as ammunition carriers in the Replacement Platoon of Ammunition Transport Unit (armored) 610.

In December 1943, after the Italian Army surrendered, 148 L 35/38 tanks were on hand, and another seventeen were built in 1944. The obsolescent vehicles were used by the Todt Organization and the police for securing operations, served the formation of several light tank units in infantry and mountain divisions in the Balkan area, and were also turned over to allied armies.

In the Captured Tank Report of December 30, 1944, 28 L 35/38 tanks were still reported by Wehrmacht units.

Above: A former Austrian M 35 tank in Wehrmacht service. The water-cooled Austrian M 07/12 machine gun has been replaced by an MG 34.

Left: M 35 small tanks, the Austrian version of the CV 33/35, and M 35 medium tanks (ADGZ) of the Austrian Army.

Above: In September 1943, the Italian Army surrendered and was disarmed by the Wehrmacht. Italian soldiers who were willing to fight, though, stayed in service with their weapons along with the Wehrmacht, as here in the 7th SS Mountain Division "Prinz Eugen", with an L 3/33 small tank marked with a German cross. (BA)

Below: Two more L 33/35 tanks in action with the 7th SS Mountain Division "Prinz Eugen" in September 1943. Through the disarming of the Italian troops in that month, the "Prinz Eugen" Division gained fifty small Italian tanks which, if usable, were distributed to the combat troops to strengthen their fighting power. (BA)

This Fiat-Ansaldo L3/33 tank is clearly marked with a German cross. These obsolescent vehicles, armed only with two machine guns, could only be used for securing duties.

Below: This L 3/33 and the L 3/35 behind it were used by a unit of the Todt Organization in 1944. The L 3/35 differed from the L 3/33 in having a riveted armor-plated box.